Dew-Drops
of the Soul

by

Yogiraj Gurunath

Siddhanath

Alight Publications

DEW-DROPS OF THE SOUL
by Yogiraj Gurunath Siddhanath

An Alight Book

Visit our website at
www.alightbooks.com

PRINTING HISTORY
First Edition / December 2001
Second Printing / November 2004
Second Edition / August 2008
Third Edition / August 2023

For information address: Alight Publications
P. O. Box 277, Live Oak California 95953.

ISBN 978-1-931833-60-8

PRINTED IN THE UNITED STATES OF AMERICA

Editor's Note

It has been over twenty years since the first publication of this unique compilation of poetic gems from a contemporary Himalayan Master, a Self-realized and perfected Being, whom we call Yogiraj Sat-Gurunath.

Gurunath has often mentioned that these " Dew-Drops of the Soul" express the essence of his inner experience and that they are the best source to learn the heights and depths of Yoga.

These "Dew-drops" are simply written in the unique way that Gurunath is able to capture the sublime in a down to earth manner for us to better understand the non-describable nature of reality.

Gurunath speaks to the soul through the doorway of the heart. He opens up our hearts so that we can attune ourselves to the reality of the True Self, in spite of the limitations of the human language and through many guises of our day-to-day experience.

Twelve of the twenty-one poems appeared in print for the first time in the first edition in 2002, while seven of them had been previously published in "Anubhuti" [1997; India]. Two new poems that appeared in the classic 'Babaji The Lightning Standing Still' have been included in this anniversary edition (2023).

For those of you who want to know more about Gurunath, you will find valuable information in the Appendix.

Turn to the "Dewdrops" and take flight on the back of the soaring Hamsa Soul-Swan.

Sat Gurunath Maharaj Ki Jay !

Table of Contents

Death

Why do people think of me,
What I am not supposed to be?
Death's cold hand they often say,
Will snatch away your earthly stay.

They call me Death and yet
I take them to eternity.
Oh this paradox of Ignorance
Deludes humanity.

Men steeped in earthly ignorance
Do dread me as their foe
Knowing not that to their Souls
The light of truth I show.

Ye Sons of Light, I am not night
Of darkness and despair
I come to save you from your woes,
Your worries and your cares.

To take you to the stillness
And that peace you often craved
That plenitude of quietude,
Land of the pure and brave.

I am the one and only way
To reach the goal sublime
Pass through my gates of Death you must
To meet your Lord Divine.

Then shun me not ye mortal men,
But Mayas dream decline
She binds you to mortality.
I to Eternal life sublime.

Rejoice then when I come to you,
Each time at end of life.
It is to take you in my arms,
From worldly storms and strife.

Then with great lovingness and care
I'll put you at His feet
Beseech of Him your cyclic ego
Never to repeat.

Such are my humble services
I offer to mankind
Do I do this for recompense?
. . . No! . . .
It's just my love that's blind!

Karma
(A Soliloquy of Mind and Spirit)

I brushed aside the curtain
Of the window of mine eye
And beheld the sparkling Truth,
That within me did reply.
Oh Man you're not this house of flesh
Which sleeps decays and dies.
You are immortal consciousness,
King of the earth and skies.

Then burdened why am I,
With this coat of flesh and bone?
I questioned earnestly that Truth,
My very conscious home.
This coat your seed desire was,
Whose fruit is now your own.
Created by yourself you must,
Reap what you have sown.

Is this also the reason
For the hardships of my life?
Yes! Each cause has its relation
Just as Husband has a Wife.
Every action its reaction has
With certainty that's True.
Do good works results of which,
Shall mould your life anew.

Pray tell me why the difference
Twixt the people on this earth?
Why do some have poverty
Some no financial dearth?
Why some sad and others gay
Some sick and others strong?
Is this the outcome of past deeds
Of personal right and wrong?

You've spoken well and seem to know
God's Mathematical Law
All wrongs must be redressed indeed,
This fact it has no flaw.
All rights are rewarded
In proportion and no more.
To each one is meted out
His exact and proper score.

This unbribable Judge we people,
Call "The Karmic Law".
The supervisor of the Fates
Of our worldly see-saw
Who justly balances the ups
And downs of lives of man
Fitting the jigsaw of our fates
As we ourselves had planned.

What proof Hamsa Atman,
Can one get of his former karma?
The proof your own existence,
Circumstances and your dharma.
Your individual present,
Tells your reciprocal past.
As per their past desires,
People get their present task.

To the Truth is Truth begot,
The liar gets his own.
So make your actions such,
Whose reactions you don't moan.
To the likeness of your thinking,
Shall your character be made.
Dig deep your mind for noble thoughts,
With intellectual spade.

Oh Hamsa Spirit of my soul
What is my final goal?
Is there any such remedy to
Break this karmic hold?
This duality of opposites,
Teach me to override.
Take me with thee oh Spirit free,
On to the other side.

I am the Sun you are my ray,
You must become the whole.
By good conduct and service,
Your character shall mould.
By devotional meditation,
I – your spirit shall unfold.
The ray become the blazing Sun,
Yourself as Me behold!

Maya

Lo is he a waking dream
Or total fallacy?
Or is she just a game of time
In God's own fantasy?

How strange this world of Maya is
How gripping and how strong
In this cosmic motion picture
The right appears all wrong.

The false appears as truth
And the truth appears all false
On this Dancing dream of Maya
Is a paradoxical waltz.

Then dance we must to nature's tune
Of lust and fame and greed
Until we realize its joys
No more than sensual feed.

Discriminate Oh Brothers mine
Between reality and dream
Life is a passing caravan
It is not what it seems.

Today we live throbbing with life.
Tomorrow we are gone
Mere shadows in a waking dream
We leave this world forlorn.

Are you this house of flesh and bone
Swayed by the senses five?
Never, you are the light of God
The honey from his hive.

You are the thinking principle
Manushya you are called
This body but a garment is
In karmic web enthralled.

Manushay is the everlasting
Principal of man
Sharir delusive Mayas child
Of perishable man.

Arise Oh Children of the Lord.
Immortal souls Divine.
Break your delusive Mayic sleep,
Race for your home sublime.

Where supremest love doth reign
Sat-Chit-Ananda by name
Who ever was even is now
Will ever by the same.

Om Tat Sat Om
Om Tat Sat Om

Hamsa Still
[The philosophy of enlightened action]

Opal Hamsa of the mystic skies
From whose bosom doth thou rise?
Where to where do flight you take
What fathomless Truth you awake !

I have no birth nor death in time
Unborn awake I never sleep
Kundali is the self-born Me
Moving creation from the deep !

My true self is the selfless Self
I came to be by Being !
Pulling the veil of Maya
By my will I am the Hamsa Still

Hamsa Eternal how may we
Being work-bound yet be everfree?
Enlightened action is the key
Which gives that final liberty!

Action from desires of the seeds
Of past or future thoughts
Creates a Karmic bondage which
Is ceaselessly with troubles fraught.

Enlightened action doth arise
Within your crystal conscious skies
Experience of the Hamsa Still
Make you know Divinity's will

If I could but with Time conspire
To relive my past life movie entire
Fashioning my future picture show
In tune with God's own mystic flow

That all pervading consciousness of stillness through eternity,
Must of necessity proclaim its ultimate reality;
Composed of nothing yet of which all else is sure composed,
It stands supreme beyond all dreams eternally reposed.

Yogiraj Gurunath

Mind Transformation

As a leaking vessel never can fill
Waters of Life so pure and still
So distracted mind fails to retain
Wisdom's nectar in its brain

To fill waters from wisdom's spring
Our minds we must to stillness bring
Then our crystal bowl of tranquil mind
With Gnosis fills of supernal kind

But if the very thoughts of mind
Be as fleeting deer and hind
Darting wayward ways they find
Such men to wisdom's ways are blind

To ease disease of random mind
A remedy suitable we must find
A rhythmic breathing tension free
With absorption the sovereign key

Steady poise the arrow your will
And shoot the fleeting mind to still
The deer of thoughts, hind & harts
Felled by your concentrated darts

As one by one they die away
Mind opens up to new day
Streams run tranquil willows sway
Here tame and gentle deer do play

Tamed and tuned to nature's flow
Mind melts into the open glow
Which radiates from the soul within
Where Wisdom's mystic fire is king!

Mystic Wine
The Bishop's Wine

Oh the Bishop's Wine by far the best
Old Vintage wine; a cut above the rest
Only he knows how to mature it best
And patiently his time invest.

Time spent in solitude of mind
Enrichens wine of any kind
Where silence stills the finest brew
That vintage tastes like honey dew.

In vermilion vestry of his mind
Brew exotic grapes of rarest kind
He culls the grape fruits fragrant Heart
No palate can ever find!

Then vermilion vintage he prepares
Within himself with breath as yeast
Ferments textured wine of sparkling zest;
Oh! The Bishop's wine by far the best!

Dew-Drops of the Soul

Each day is holy communion day
For a Bishop of my mindless stay
I drink I'm drunk I drift away
A euphoria blows me heavens way

The holy grail my crystal thought
Holds my vermilion wine sublime
I sip I seep humanity's heart
Knowing it to be my heart at large!

From sanctum-torium drop by drop
Tongue soaks elixir's wine sublime.
Lulls me to ecstasy's rosy rest
Oh! The Bishop's wine by far the best

Hallelujah Christ is risen today
Wake up Bishop, it's Easter day
Your wine has had its winning way
Hosannas here with us to stay!

Ode To Surya
(A Solar Meditation)

I drink oh drink thee Sun of Life
Your roaring radiance rinse me through
Gushing through spine with Sizzling joy
I thy Divinity enjoy!

From thy elysian fountain rays
I drink immortal Pranic Life
Rejuven Body and my mind
Dissolve all worldly woe and strife!

Dancing with thine immortal light
Each cell suffused with joy of Life
I glorify this gift oh Lord
No Emperor ever can afford!

Orange elixirs wine sublime
Flows glows in every fiber mine
Filling me with thy Bliss sublime
Making me to My Self Divine!

Déjà Vu

Wild flowers so fresh in life
Breeze through alleys of my mind
Fragrancing memories of the past
In mountain lakes reflections cast

In wooded valleys berries crushed
The flavor of the mystic musk
Within me did old memories rise
Devotions to the sunset skies

Forest aroma deep in damp
Wild smell of the wooded pines
Oh ! the déjà vu of jungle times
Of long past meditations lives

Where in sylvan bowers I sat
Not in this world nor in that
Just in the joy of Selfing mirth
The odor of the fragrant earth !

My mind a laughing gurgling stream
Running the bedrocks mossy green
Becomes a calm meandering dream
Flowing into Myself serene

My melting mind a flowing stream
Entered the rainbow ocean light
There was no fear nor sorrows night
Except awareness and delight

How long I sat there no one knows
The eventide its shadows cast
In many a sunrise rays I basked
No one came nor ever asked

The trivial round the common task
Meditation then to me became
A natural mind in tune so tame
Transcending frivolous name and fame

Just being quiet was so good
A lying log, a forest wood
Moving with the natural breeze
Amidst the deep dark forest trees

With body dead consciousness live
Expanding in eternal skies
Beyond mayas conditioned dream
The self merging in Self supreme.

My Cup of Tea

The morning sunshine on my back
Gentle breezes blowing through
Gold brown books on the old wood rack
Oh! My steaming cup of tea that brew!

From which mysteriously did spring
Nostalgic memories old and new
Wafting my mind aloft and light
To another worldly inner flight

Of mystic flavors colors too
Of which never ever knew
Yet somehow from my inner most Being
I experienced True what I was seeing

A Bliss experienced oft before
It satisfied my innermost core
Knowing it to be myself and more
Of my own larger treasure store

All things were made of spiritual light
Swans lake to lake in glorious flight
Fainting fragrance Lotus bloomed
In this Paradise the mind was doomed

Thoughts die dissolve to live in knowing
That boundless consciousness all growing
In ever expanding Love and Joy
All things of matter but a toy

A figment of the conscious Self
Conditioned mind a sneaky elf
Of negativity in time
Was transformed to Gnosis sublime

Heard it but I didn't hear
The dog barking so far so near
In the backyard chasing hens
Fluttering hither to the fence

The neighboring housewife I beheld
Brisk and about her daily chores
Washing dishes cleaning floor
Sweeping in and out of doors

Yet all my consciousness was me
In spite of all this revelry
Immersed in my awareness me
Bound to worldly task yet Free

Fame nor position matter
To one's inner life of peace
Virtues used as virtues sake
Cause all sorrows to cease

Autobiography of the Self

●

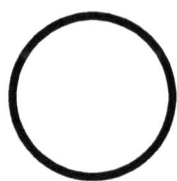

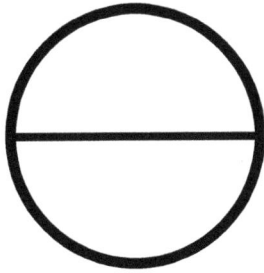

*Boundless lay the Self existent
in the Paramartha of the Self,
Spread beyond Infinity, from Eternity to Eternity,
was perfect absolute and calm;
calm undisturbed, for
Creation was not yet conceived of the Creator
who in the stillness of His Majesty did reign.*

Parinishpanna art though Oh All-in-All,
Not this, Not this thou art,
the essence of all light and dark
There was no darkness then,
there even was no light
There was no action then to cause reaction, all was
Thyself ineffable and endless consciousness of Bliss

For then in nothing was the everything,
in everything was nothing
These feeble words seek humbly
to express Thy majesty Para Brahman
For even Absolute is limited
to the Oh ineffable peace
That passeth all understanding.

TRUTH, the life of Prana lay potential in Thee,
Oh All-In All
Time was not, Space was not,
Creation there was none.
Yet Oh Supreme, all were held
in Thy bosom of Duration
The Lord of LIGHT had not awakened but
reposed in Thee.

The Eternal Spark had not impulsed
to set causation in motion;
Then would the birth of creation begin
in Relative Sequence
And Maha Maya would go forth
in her celestial dance
Creating Countless universes and galaxies to
Thy Glory.

If at one time, at the same place,
that very moment
The sunburst of a countless suns occur.
That brilliance would scarce suffice to show Thy shadow
What must be Thy light!
Darker than the darkest hell; more glorious
than Brahma Lok art Thee
Thy splendor knows no majesty.

Lo! Thou didst exhale Thy universal Self,
Oh Calm
and Thy Infinite Mind Oh Lord
did make the mighty Lord of Flame
Who exploding in His Light
did Maya's Creation ignite
To set the Wheel of Creation in Motion,
Maya's Motion.

The eternal Mother Adi-Shakti then did
make her galaxies
and other relative aspects of creation did begin,
The Sound Sublime, creator of causation space and time
did originate in Thy bosom Oh Thou
Mula-Prakriti of Light
Resounding in every substance
of creation Thy organ Oooommmm!

Then Light and heat and moisture,
they were born of Thee
Oh! Mother Adi-Shakti,
Vast Nebulae of light and heat did float
the spaces infinite to regulate themselves into galaxies
Then by Myriad Permutation Combinations Mother
Did Thou form the Suns and Stars in
Thy immortal Song.

Great masses of vibrating incandescent light were stars
So large as to stagger human imagination
Mother really dost though wear such jewels
on Thy breast?
And still find time to love us mortal children so far below
Oh Bhagavati,
in every molecule Thy love it glows and grows.

These mighty vapors of Light and the Stars
they stud Thy brow
Oh Thou Mother of Eternal Light
Thy glory knows no night
These children galaxies of Thine,
these Stellar Solar systems hold;
in perfect harmony they move,
all held by that force
Oh Mother we mortals call Thy Radh,
Thy gravitational love.

Then came the Sons of light - of Shakti they were born,
Blazing in their power and truth they worked
through worlds and stars and fraught
cooling the hot, heating the cold, moistening the dry
and perfecting in their harmony
all undue disharmony to
set about the perfect evolution
of the Worlds of mortal man.

The Cyclic Motion of Creation then began,
it was causation's dance in relative Oceans
The day came on and gave birth unto the night
The breeze raced over vast tracts of solid lands
and liquid waters
did their position take in hollows of the earth.

Sacred Bhumi
oh Mother World Thou art;
the essence of Adi-Shakti;
To Thee, by whose womb we mortals were born
our endless salutations to Thee
Oh Thou divine spouse of Vishnu, our eternal Lord
Our Universe of Endless stars lives their lifes in Thee
Only so long as Thou dost wish them to be.

Oh *Bhumi Ma*, *Thy* chosen child was *Vasundhara*
Who came to be so that she may mother her
mortal living *Man*.
Then did begin the evolution of the future *Man*
that spark of life divine entered the mineral rock,
its first primeval home.
For the spark was of *Vasundhara*
the Child of *Bhumi*
Who in turn was of *Adi-Shakti Parameswari*.

And Mother Adi-Shakti,
one with Mula-Prakritri was of
the Essence of Parinishpanna,
our Supreme Paramatma.
Then that spark of life was also of the Paramatma in the
relative sense.
There was nothing not of Paramatma,
the Supreme Purusha.

The spark divine grew from the mineral rock
into the plant
Wherein it did flourish,
then dying out from the plant the Spark of life
was born into the fish and then the mammals.
I died from the lower tabernacle of matter
to enter a more expressive One.

I died out from the rock to live in the plant.
I died out from the plant to live in the fish and reptile.
I died from reptile to live in animal and lastly
I died out from the animal house of flesh
to enter the house of man.
Wherein did I become the lessor by dying?
For dying was another form of life.

And all along Evolution's path did I travel,
My outer coats were different,
each one more expressive than the first
but essentially I was the same.
And finally awaited me
the most crucial temple, Man
But it was only a man of clay,
until I entered my ray.

I entered into the flesh of man as ray of light,
the thinking light,
I was that consciousness who came
from the Supreme.
My Light gave the house of flesh to know
that I was a glow the child of light.
The Ego it was formed by me
for future generations to be
the thinking principle they know as mind
which is the essence of all Mankind.

I came into the physical house of man,
to rule over that Tabernacle of flesh,
but was deluded by the Satanic desires of the Flesh
into thinking I was a body and not the light.
This Heresy of separateness covered my sight,
forgetting I was potentially divine,
Maya's veil covered that spark to haunt me in
the darkness of body flesh.

Then man looked up to the portending stars
to question whether they his life did make.
The stars looked down, smiled and replied
"Son, nothing can Thy Immortal Essence take."
Then girding up His Loins the cave man did begin
his upward evolution aspiring to be one with
Him who is in all and break Mayic illusion.

Oh Maya Thou nature's eve,
Thou didst hide from my Manus Self,
my Father Self the Atman Buddhi.
Then my struggle of life began
to unite Manus that was me
to my Father Atma Buddhi and Jivan mukta to be;
The Cyclic ego then began
its rounds of reincarnations.

It did repeat itself till Manu's Son
vanquished Satanic Maya
and did become one with father Atma-Buddhi.
Who essentially one with Paramartha was
The Father Atma, Mother Buddhi and
Manu's Child being one.
The deluded Manusputra
had regained his lost birth-right
and entered into his Father -Mother bosom of Light.

The fallen state regained: Lo!
Behold the lesser ones to come.
The lower animals had to struggle up.
Oh Sons of light help them! Guide them!
The plants, the rocks must be evolved
for in all was the essential spark of Atman.
The Paramatmic Divine Self must help
the Jivatmic human Self.
This is the Cosmic Law.

The molecules in each mineral substance did contain
vast quantity of atoms, each representing
a miniature Solar System.
All rotating revolving and evolving
as per a preplanned power
That ineffable mighty essence of the Self Atma.
From the Vastest Nebulae to the Atoms smallest spray
did He in His own majesty parade.

The Spirit was the essence of the All,
both big and small,
Hot and cold, light and dark did contain
that one essential spark.
Even the minute electron contained
its essence positrons
that were composed of mesons
whose energy children
lifetrons traveled through the breath of man.

*But finer than the lifetrons of Prana was the
Essence of God-thought,
one with the all-pervading Spirit, the Atman.
There was no segregation in this Spirit of God-thought,
For from this the dream fabric of Maya
was composed and made
It was the vastest infinity of Divinity.*

From the essential substance of God thought
the Sun and the Moon and the Stars were built,
Stellar and Solar Systems also had their sway
because God thought was in them to stay.
All was of God's thought
and God-thought was One thought,
The divine thought of
the universal oneness of Eternity.

For being the subtlest of the all
from it was made the all;
It was the smallest of the small far
beyond human imagination.
Would it then be correct to call that
God-thought non-Being?
And thereby express its absolute entirety
over creation in Being?

The All-being was the God-thought which was
the essential essence of every atom of creation.
The all being was the God-thought
Self-existent in Eternity.
The Self that all pervading
consciousness of stillness through eternity
Composed of nothing yet
of which all else is sure composed,
It stands supreme beyond all dreams eternally reposed.

Spirit is the God-thought, there is nothing it is not.
The All is One, the One is all, the All-in All Paramartha,
Oh, Absolute Majesty of sublimest existence,
Oh ineffable peace beyond human understanding,
Our ceaseless salutation to Thee
who ever was, even is now and shall forever be.

Let not precious moments slip by
Seek now ! the ultimate truth
Jivahamsa spread your wings to fly
Immortal realms which death defy

My Mother of Renunciation

I am thy child, Oh Panna Dai,
a countless deaths I'll die for thee
Oh Mother of True sacrifice,
Thy courage knows no majesty.

I love thee more than all the Mothers
past and yet to be
Give me thy courage Ma and
teach me how a Tyagi I must be.

What greater courage could
a nursing Mother ever show
Than sacrifice her very throbbing
blood and heart and soul.

Oh Mother, Thou didst wrench me
from thy breast I had not drunk
That love I so much craved you kept,
I empty did depart.

Thy urge to give me nectar of thy love,
it was so strong
That 'ere my lips had left thy breast
thy love it did gush forth.

Then from thy breast did Maya flow,
and heart renunciations glow
Thy milk did drench thy clothes Oh Ma,
and dripping sadly to the floor it begged

"Leave me not my Child for thee
I love much more than me."
But Mothers blood of sacrifice
rebuked her very milk and cried.

"Hold me not back to renounce
every molecule and ounce of love,
For I must give so that the Nation's
countless children, they may live."

But Mother you still owe me love
which is by birthright mine
From you I have to learn as yet
the Greatest lesson of all time.

That lesson and that Truth Oh Mother
still remains in breast of Thine.
Then let me be once more of thee
and drink my fill of sacrifice.

Oh Panna Dai, that which was thine
was also ever mine
That milk of sacrifice and Tyag had courage
and had love Divine.

Not even bravest of the brave
can teach me to renounce
Only from thy mayic milk I'll learn
to break all Maya's bounds.

My heart in thee, Thy soul in me
such oneness did us bind
Then How did you my loving heart
surpass all humankind?

The pain of separation was much more
for thee than twas for me
Bhagvati of Tyag art thou,
who else could bear such agony.

Yes Mother now I know,
none else than Bhagvati art thou
To sacrifice your heart and blood,
the kingdom's honor to restore.

I felt thee gently with firm hands
lay me in my death bed
The brute did stab his steel in me
and Mother's love ran red.

That blood which flowed with love of Tyag,
it glowed.
My Mother's blood,
the highest of renunciation showed.

I thought by giving me to death
you had left me and gone
But little did I know Oh Ma,
death was your other form.

Then I let my body go even
as a snake leaves slough
To enter once again into
my Mother's conscious womb and glow.

*Upon strength of such sacrifice a
re myriad heroes born.
My ceaseless salutations are to thee,
My Mother, and my all.*

*Thy manifested Self Oh Ma
in form and flesh was Panna Dai
Thy Self in true they only knew
who passed the gates of death in time.*

*Koti Koti Pranams
Koti Koti Pranams*

Prayer to Kundalini Divine

Hiss Kundali sting ego mine
With nectar poison so sublime
Piercing my rainbow Lotus shrines
Making me to myself divine !

Kundalini bless me with thy blaze
Delusion, suffering fear efface
Spine darkness; with they lightening light
Fragrance me ! Negative karma ignite!

You are livingness ! its Life you keep
Oh Mother of the mystic deep!
Remove shadow of death from me
In Shiva deathlessly to be!

Yogi

Living in Calm and Solitude
Subduing body and his Mind
Within himself in gratitude
Ridding Desires of all Kind.

Neath Sylvan bowers in his Seat
Cool Stream flows by deerskin laid neat
This is the Yogi's true retreat
In meditation is his treat.

The Asans selected best are two
For him to meditation do
The first Padmasana lotus trance
Then Siddhasana the perfect stance.

Yogi's in Dhyan become aware
How breath at birth did them ensnare
Twenty one thousand thirty score
Japa leads soul to salvation's door.

In Padmasan do bandh trine
Focus on Kundalini in spine
Practice breathing Pran-apan
Know precious Kundalini Gyan.

By Hard Practice sweat beads form
Rub them into the body form
Then Yogi must of milk avail
Avoid all food, acid and stale.

Food is energy for the mind
And goes to mental making
Soft sweets and fruits oh! Yogi eat
At every fast of breaking

For psychic nerves to Purify
One must move both sun and moon
And all humours is us to dry
We must perfect maha-mudra try

Hamsa is Gayatri's ajapa japa
Opener of Yogi's heavenly door
Breathing with awareness let him strive
And let not him his animal drive

From Kundali is Hamsa born
Flowing is spine as Pran-apan
Yogi's stilling the Pran-apan
Are true adepts in sama Dhyan.

This knowledge is all supreme
It's practice melts the magic dream
Experience of the "Hamsa Still"
Makes Us know Divinity's will.

Oh valiant Yogi striving free
By pranic kumbak break the seal
The Brave by storm the heaven's take
Nirvan through kundali they make

Having blocked with her face
The path leading to Shiva's shrine
Awake! Oh Kundalini mine
And lead me to my home divine!

The Yogic Prana ablaze unites
With Kundalini to ignite
Mind intellect then penetrate
Sukhma chakras living light

She like a hissing serpent goes
Glistening kundali upward flows
By magnet heat of Pranayam
Awaken's she! Our wisdom grows.

Your own meat swallow yogi
Get drunk with inner wine
The profane value these secrets not
Cast not your pearls before the swine.

By Allakh Gorakhia's mystic touch
Disease hunger not sleep assail
Yogis who rent mayas death veil
Are those who in khechari prevail

By afflictions is he troubled not
Nor tainted by his fruits of karma
Is troubled not by sting of death
He Mrityunjay conqueror of breath

Take padmasana perfect pose
In lush serene surrounding
Shivnetra Yogi lost in OM
Know self as sound Resounding

Om thou creative light divine
In all the seven heavens shine
Lightless light of all the light
Sun moon and fire you ignite

In the Blueprint of creation
Emblazoned is thy cosmic seal
Causation space & time are but
Projections of your magic dream

Om with every breath & thought
Sets yogi free from karma
Giving Nirvana to striving souls
As per their own swadharms

Even the evil chanting 'Om'
Are tainted not by karma
They will be like a lotus lying
Unwet in water and undying

Absorbed in Om, the semen stills
By ceaseless Pranayama
Lifeprana is still, semen is still
Conquer death, new life fulfill

Yogiraj Gurunath

As long as pran in body flows
The soul therein doth reside
Pran leaves, soul also body leaves
So live for God! Do Pranayam

To ward off kala death they say
Gods and sages in Pranayam stay
Yogi puts death's fear away
And lives in prana the kevali way

Deathless Yogi, fearless bold
Prana between the eyebrows hold
By kevali in Shivanetra be!
Oh death where is they victory?

In lotus posture yogi stay
Do sun-moon prana of night & day
Spinal breathing it is called
Victor of death be breath enthralled

He stands supreme beyond all dream
Of friend and foe alike
Success 'n failure, name and fame
To Him a mere dolls wedding game

Satisfied with what he has
Bathing in wisdom's fountain head
Conqueror of the senses five
He drinks the honey from his hive

In joy and sorrow light & dark
He ever that eternal spark
In honour and dishonour too
The constant yogi ever new!

The well-made mind is Self alone
Its wrongs need no atone
Because the well-made mind shall soar
Above karmic effect and flaw

Established in the Self he glows
Beyond intelligence he flow's
Transcending all the senses five
In the "here-now!" Truth alive

Beholding self by Self supreme
Shattering the waking dream
Maya shall be put to flight
By those who in the Self delight

Yogiraj Gurunath

A Compassionate & healing light
A Hamsa in its slendid flight
Away oh darkness! Fly oh night!
The Yogi comes in radiant might.

Allak Niranjan Om Shiv Om!!
Allak Niranjan Om Shiv Om!!

The sunset shades of melting hue,
white maimed clouds rolled home.
The violet canopies heavenly vault,
melts in the self-same dome

If at one moment time and place,
the sun burst of a countless suns occurred,
this would scarce suffice to show thy shadow.
Oh lord what must be thy light.

Reality

This world is but a thoughtfulness
of Mayic atoms intertwined
Whose electrons are energy
of light essence sublime.

Newton rediscovered and
declared the Laws of Motion
Sir Apple fell for Eve before
and then for Gravitation

Cause and effect are bound to be
one with nature's duality
Oscillating within the laws
of Mayas' karmic causality.

What physics and what chemistry
their laws must have corollary
Action reaction, attraction repulsion,
cause and effect are bound to be.

Laws of creation subject are
to equilibrium forces.
This world in balance cannot be
without its gains and losses.

> *There is no day without its night,*
> *nor cause without effect*
> *For attraction must repulsion be*
> *just as for life is death.*

The Einstein based his theory
on hypothesis of light
Relating all that matters
to finality of light.

> *But the Krishna and the Christ perceived*
> *light to be form of energy.*
> *Emanating from the omniscient mind*
> *that one cosmic reality.*

They further saw that energy
was not the final law.
It was a grosser consciousness
but that too had its flaw.

This world our sages did perceive
is mindstuff materialized.
In relative sequence it is built
deceiving mortal eyes.

All that is composed they knew
must get decomposed
Where then does reality lie?
All matter being composed.

That all pervading consciousness
of stillness through Eternity
Must of necessity proclaim
its ultimate reality.

Composed of nothing yet of which
all else is sure composed
It stands supreme beyond all dreams
eternally reposed.

That one cosmic reality
is spirit they perceived
Whose omnipresent essence
is everlasting bliss.

Whose one dream atom
doth our universe contain
Its myriad worlds and planets
He doth orderly maintain.

To This Everlasting Truth of Love,
This Infinite Divinity
Countless creations homage pay
throughout His Own Eternity.

Dedicated to
Shiv Goraksha Nath
Babaji

Who art Thou?
I know Thee not and yet I am of Thee
I cannot comprehend thee,
Oh Thou Emperor of Divinity.

I sit and melt in silence of
Thy Love Oh Infinite.
Make me thy Truth,
Make me thy Love
Eternal Lord of Light

Countless creations do you make
Goraksha Nath Divine
A thought projected by you
Makes causation, space and time

There never was a Sage or Saint
Who was not born of Thee
Thou art the essence of their Souls
Divine Paramatma Free

We Jivatmas also Lord
Have our birth and being in Thee
The Thou must also be in us
Supremest Monarchy.

How shall I love Thee Babaji?
Words are so dry and dumb
I can't express Thy majesty
My intellect runs numb.

My heart it bursts oh all in all
To love Thee endlessly
But Lord I cannot bring to words
I'm tongue-tied hopelessly.

Give me the strength to shout Thy love
Across the seven seas
Deludging this world with light
For infinite eternities.

In solitudes of my mind
My devotion it dost burst to hear
Thy song immortal song of love
Thou everlasting Seer.

As long as darkness covers me
And ignorance doth do us part
So long in agony I'll be
Striving to be with Thee my Heart.

Through pain and hunger I shall strive
To touch Thy feet oh Lord
It matters not if bones or body
Perish in this battle fort.

I'm burning in My love for Thee
Eternal infinite
I cannot rest in peace now
Till I do become thy Light.

In silent supplications
I do burn and yearn to be in Thee
Hear Thou my soul cry
Break my bonds Babaji
Set me free.

Set me free to be in Thee
Let there be none of me
Then me in Thee
Thy love in me
I shall become of Thee.

Pleasures nor palaces exude
That Bliss of peaceful solitude
Attunement with the Self alone
Gives that final beatitude !

Sat Guru Bhakti

From the Guru's feet flows the
spiritual river Ganga
Which washes all the sins of my Heart
Oh Shiva when shall my relationship
With you become one?

> The love that flows from the Guru's Eyes
> Saturates my body with Nectar.
> Oh Shiva when shall my relationship
> With you become one?

The Guru's blessing flame awakens me
And opens the eyes of my heart and soul
Oh Shiva when shall my soul be
Merged in Thy eternal Spirit?

> A blinding light in my mental sky
> May I behold Shiv Goraksha
> All my binding shackles of Karma are broken

One with Shiva I have become
All my attachments are broken
And One with Shiva I have become.

ALAK NIRANJAN KAR SHIVOM!
ALAK NIRANJAN KAR SHIVOM!

Thy Love Lives Oh Christ

Who feels Thy love Beloved Christ,
it spreads into eternity
It permeates each atom
our existing Humanity.

Each fibre in my body and
my innermost spirit yearns for Thee
In what fashion shall I Lord!
Express my burning love for Thee.

Words are too callous and too dry
to touch thy ineffable Love Divine.
Speak to me Jesus in my heart
and tell me Thou art mine.

Such is the depth and warmth of
Thy ineffable love divine.
Speak to me Jesus in my heart
and tell me thou art mine.

Tell me Oh Christ; That I am Thine
I ask for nothing more
Beyond all riches and all fame
do I Thy love adore.

Oh Messiah of the humble and
the meek and pure in heart
I yearn to be absorbed
in Thee never to depart.

While suffering pangs on cross of death;
Divinity it spoke from you
"Father forgive these children
for they know not what they do".

Was there a loftier love phrase
ever uttered by mankind?
Saying this Thou didst depart,
leaving Thy body coat behind.

Oh King of Yogis little did
these blinded children know
That Thou were master of
Thy body and its passing show!

Then brighter than brilliance itself
on Easter Thou didst rise
To show the Light of love divine
to blinded mortal eyes.

Then Heaven and earth rejoiced
for the Spirit of the Lord
Had filled creation with its love
and struck through Thee that cord.

That cord of Love which doth vibrate
the human fibre up to date
And make us cry with love and joy:
Hosanna in the Highest!

Hari Om Tat Sat Om

Then stiller than stillness itself
With bated breath, I do behold
The rising Self-Sun's nectar gold
I dissolve in that mystery untold.

The Gaatha
In Glory of Goraksha

Deathless splendor fearless bold
Goraksha the living lightning holds
Savior of gods and human kind
Liberates them from the karmic grind

The son of Shiva and Parvati
Goraksha in Ganesha Goshti
Being Shiva himself in formless form
Taught Ganesha Samadhi of Divinity

From Your sacred fire did You take
The potent ashes of Your Dhuni
And gave it to Vishnu and Brahma
Creation to again remake

You battled the Goddess of Hingalaaja
And freed her from mayic mirage
To Datta you gave his mantra as draum
Enlightened him to its origin from Om

Hanumana and Bhima at territory war
You pacified both and settled the score
First testing Arjuna by killing the bore
Then gifting him with the Gandiva bow

To Mary the gift of Christ You bestowed
In Gabriel's apparel You were clothed
It is written in the books of Dabisthana
To the Prophet You gave knowledge of gyana

Shiva born the disciple of Macchendra yogi
Took the name of Goraksha Mahayogi
Steered Macchendra off the mayic tryst
Illumined and melted his karmic mist

Desires for golden palace by Bharthari
You fulfilled in the incarnation of Lahiri
Chowringee disciple of Goraksha Ishwara
Reincarnated as Yogi Yukteshwar

The glories of Krishna did Meera sing
But her life and living to Goraksha bring
He did Alam Prabhu's ignorance efface
And showed to him Goraksha's God-own face

Kabir was born as Yogi Sri Chandra
Then Lahiri the conqueror of Indra
Vikramaditya was your disciple true
Born as Siddhanath Kriya work to do

To Ramananda the joy of Rama you gave
To Kabir the Kriya Yoga of prana
To Nanak you gave the true Sat-nam
Irradiant Lord beyond death and grave

The king of mystics was Gyannath
Initiated by brother Nivrittinath
Who in turn was blessed by Gahninath
Your kundalini disciples on yogic path

In Gorakpur was Yogananda born
He was chosen for the yogic norm
Sent by Sri Yukteshwar to the west
To spread Kriya Yoga and to do his best

Goraksha Shataka

Namo Namah Guru Supreme
Thy presence shatters mayas dream.
Thy glory, us knowledge to know
Transforming us in bliss to grow !

Constant in thy swayambhu light.
Raj hansa in thy splendid flight.
Beyond causation space and time
Homage minnath guru sublime.

With devotion having homage payed
Goraksha opens liberations path
Secret fusion of head and heart
Yogis where by to bliss depart.

To benefit Yogis of all kind
Nath unveils the mindless mind,
With hundred gems beyond all price
Dispelling ignorance in a trice.

This gyan inverts the senses five …
…from Mayic pull to spiritual hive.
Beyond the gates of death he glides
Yogi who in Gorak confides.

Oh Valiant Yogi striving free
Practice Yoga and Siddha be
Benedictions of yogis divine
Dispelling sorrow ... on you shine.

Asan and Pranayam gems sublime
Pratyahara Dharna jewel the self
The fifth the diamond dhyan divine
Then flowers Samadhi beyond time.

Asans many as beings there be
Beyond the ken of humanity
Shiva alone knows the family tree
Whose blossoms blooming set us free.

Eighty four lacs the asans they say
Expounded by Nath in every way
But he specially selected eighty four
To pave the way salvations door.

Then he further selected asans two
For collecting of the honey dew.
The first the Siddha perfect stance
The second Yogis lotus trance.

Siddhasana opens salvation door
Left heel against perineum floor
The right against the kanda squeeze
Eyes in bhrukuti and then freeze.

Kamalasan conquers death disease
Right foot on left thigh with ease
With left foot do the same as this
And steady glide into the Bliss !

How can yogis . . . Yogis be ?
Who knows not centers ; Nadis tree.
16 adharas and sheaths five
Must know to in divinity dive.

This body temple with doors nine
Upheld by spinal pillar fine
Presiding shaktis five sublime
Yogi know them to be divine.

The mula is four, swadhistan six,
Manipur has ten petals fixed
Emblazoned in the heart of Prana
Twelve anhata petals shine in dhyan.

Vishuddha sixteen petalled blue
Agyana quicks - Hamsa flight anew ;
Sahasrara the 1000 petalled sun
In its splendors second to none.

The muladhara is base and root
Followed next by swadistan
Between them kamrupa yonisthan
Place for kula kundalini Dhyan

The chatur prana chakra adhara
The root and rhythm of Sangsara
Above which doth the yoni be
Praise by adepts as "lover's eye"

Irradiant linga didst yoni stands
Bejewelled splendor facing back
Yogis who actualize this light
Are masters of immortal might!

Yonisthan of molten gold
Triangular lightning flash!
Doth house of Kundalini fold
Whose virgin radiance never old.

Having seen the light supreme
Yogi transforms the mayic dream
With Alakh! Samadhi now he glows…
…beyond the birth death cycle goes.

By word of (sva) doth pran arise
And raises Hamsa to the skies
The resting pran in Swadisthan
From which is named the Medhra sthan.

To sushumna the kanda is strung
Like a threaded jewel hung.
This region of the navel called
Manipur where samana installed.

The soul doth wander till it finds
Anahata nada beyond the mind
Then rested in the self remains
Beyond merit demerit twain.

The seventy two thousand nadis born
From the Kanda yoni pran,
Located twist the navel and…
…the Linga Yoni sthan

Among the thousands of nadis
Seventy two are selected chief
From them the most important sthan,
Given to ten vehicles of Prana.

Ida, Pingala, Sushumna three
Chief nadis of evolutions tree.
Then hastajivhava, gandhari
With Pusa and Yashasvini.

Alambusa Kuhus and Samhini
Are the vital nadis ten.
All yogis having knowledge of
Should learn their location then.

Ida runs left Pingala up right
Sushma in mid region reigns.
Awaiting kundalini's light
Left eye ganhari moon of night.

Hastjiva the sunlight in the right eye
Pusha hears pranava in the right ear
While Yashashvini resides left ear
Alambusa gives vach siddhi clear.

Kuhus nadi joins linga sthan
Samkhini carries mula prana
Such are the vital nadis ten
Giving us light again and again.

Conductors of prana are nadis three
Ida, Pingala and Sushumni,
With their presiding deities three
Sun, Moon, and Fire Kundalini.

Prana inhales, apan exhales
Saman digests, Udan regulates.
Vyan, Naga Kurma in body flow
There Deodatta Krhara Dhananjay glow.

Hridaya prana Gudadal apan
Positive negative poles of dhyan
Navel saman the throat udana
And spreading the body rosy vyana.

Prana is life, apan is death
Saman stores food assimilates
Udan is life's metabolic key
Vyan flows throughout our body free.

Then comes secondary pranic life
Naga, Kurma and krkara energy
With Devdatta second to prana
And Dhananjay following Vyana.

And though the body lifeless be
Dhanajay leaveth not the tree
These pranas ten, and nadis ten
Match one another n all men.

Soul is struck by Pran Apan
Spines up and down salvations path.
The life of breath is death indeed
Upon whose victory Yogis feed.

The jiva controlled by pran apan
Is restless with no samadhan
Moving in Ida Pingalasthan
It cannot be perceived in dhyan.

As a Hamsa soars in azure blue skies
Our consciousness to the heavens flies
But bound by the gunas three
Prana apan hold wings of liberty!

The Prana Apanic Anusandhan
Mastered by Yogic Pranayam
Brings union of these Vayus two
Sets free the (Hamsa's) flight anew.

The Jiva's pran exhaled with "Ha"
And apan inhaled with "Sa"
Ever doth the Soul breath say
The Hamsa mantra night and day.

Yogis in dhyan become aware
How breath at birth did them ensnare
Twenty one thousand thirty score
Japa leads soul to salvations door.

Hamsa is Gayatris ajapa japa
The opener of yogis moksha dvar
So with sincerity let him strive
And let not him his animal drive.

This knowledge is all supreme,
Its practice melts the magic dream
The experience of the "Hamsa Still"
Makes us know the cosmic will.

From kundali is Gayatri born
Who then becomes the Pran
Yogis uniting Pran-apan
Are true adepts in sama dhyan.

   Above our kanda in coils eight
   Kundalini seals the yogis fate
   with head resting at Brahmadvar
   She our salvations tavanhara.

Having blocked with her face
The path leading to Shivas shrine
Awake ! oh sleeping splendour mine
And lead me to my home divine !!

   The yogic prana ablaze unites
   with kundalini to ignite
   Mano – buddhi then penetrate
   Sushmna chakras living light.

She like a hissing serpent goes
Glistening kundali upwards flows
By magnet heat of pranayam
Awakens She ! our wisdom grows.

Oh valiant yogi striving free
By pranic kumbhak break the seal !
The brave by storm the heavens take
Nirvana through Kundalini they make.

In padma asan do tri – bandh
Focus on kundali in kanda
Do the Hamsa pran apan
Gain precious kundalini gyan.

Hard practice, beads of sweat form,
Rub them into the body form
Then yogi must of milk avail
Avoid all food acid and stale.

Yogi immersed in yog abhyas
Must channel senses and be chaste.
Dwelling far from worldly bhog
Makes yogi master of Yoga.

Food is fodder for the mind
And goes to mental making
Eat sweet and soft mitahar
At every fast of breaking.

Eight coiled kundali on kanda
Gives mukti to yogis sincere
And bondage to the manda
So those who practice need not fear.

  Yogis who ready for mukti
  Khechari, mahamudra masters be
  Jalandhar, Uddiyan and Mula bandh
  Adepts be, to break mayic skanda.

With all the nadis purified
The moving of both Sun and Moon
And all the humors in us dried
Is perfect maha mudra done.

  Pressing perineum with left heel
  Inhale then stretch the right side feet
  Hold breath go forward and touch toe
  Repeat left centre each breath let go.

Having practiced with jyotsna moon
And then equal with bhaskar sun
This mudra should be done
By daily practice our well being.

For him no food is good or bad
Who does the maha mudra
Food poisoning, foods of defect
Will on him have no ill effect.

Ills like consumption, leprosy
Away from such a yogi flee
Who true to maha mudra be
In regular sadhana practice.

The bringer of success to those
Whom mahamudra is so close
Must only be to the wise disclosed
Souls sincere calm and reposed.

Daily eat cow flesh yogi pure
Get lost in wine and revelry
When dazed and dazzled in the eye
Be free ! by khechari roam the sky.

By Allakh ! Gorakhias magic touch
Disease hunger nor sleep assail
Yogis who rent mayas death veil
Victors who in khechari prevail.

By afflictions is he troubled not
Nor tainted by his fruits of Karma
Is not troubled by sting of death
Deathless He, conqueror of breath

Precious and prized by all adepts
The chitta enters Khe the sky
Tongue frees mind of bondage thoughts
Unmani brings to all souls lost.

By Bindu our body composed
Of flesh and blood and bone
By Bindu it is decomposed
When essence withdraws home.

Who seal by khechan Bindu gem
Embraced by damsels of the spheres
Their bindu fallenth not to waste
For they immortal soma taste.

So long as Khechari mudra done
The bindu falls not down
As long as bindu up remains
Death dies Yogi immortal reigns.

Yogiraj Gurunath

By chance, should bindu descend
And move towards the yoni sthan
It is arrested and returned
By shakti of yon mudra dhyan.

The vital bindu is two kinds
Pure white and blood red
The first is called semen virile
The blood red, menstrual.

Rajus the female flows from sun
Bindu the male secrets from moon
Difficult fusion of these two
Evolves you to dimensions new.

Bindu of Shiva, rajas of Shakti
Bindu is indu and rajas ravi
Unite these elements by alchemy
In alakh Niranjan be ever free !

Then by shakti chalan vayu
Rajas impelled to join bindu
Volatile wonderful the union be
Then you Yourself as divinity see.

122

Then (Bindu) with Chandra is one
And rajas with ravee unites
But a yogi true is only he
Who marrying both gets karma free.

Kala the great garuda keeps flying
Past barriers of decay and death
So uddiyan immortal lion slays
Beaths elephant to make life days.

Practice then the uddiyan bandh
Awaken kundali of kanda
By ceaseless study of this art
Yogis to mukti dham depart.

Jalandar is the chin lock
And practiced to prevent the moon
Letting its nectar flow to waste
Giving yogis sanjeevanis taste.

By closing the throat in Jalandar
The nectar in the head contained
Unconsumed by bodies death fire
And life serene in the self remains.

Third lock is called Mula Bandh
Apan withdraw then rectum close
Press yoni with back of left heel
And then enter the yogic pose.

By pran apanic anusandhan
Purified are inner body sthans
Even the aged and the old
By mula get young and bold.

Take padmaasan perfect pose
In lush serene surrounding
Shivnetra Yogi lost in Om
Know self as nada resounding.

Om thou supreme light divine
In worlds bhur, bhava, svaha shine
Light of light that lights all lights
Sun moon and fire you ignite.

Father of the triform time
Of past present and future
Contained in thee all Gods and worlds
Om's light doth feed all nature.

In thee desire and knowledge grow
Rudri, Brahmi, Vaishnavi flow.
Such art thou ineffable light
Om splendour of the lightless light.

In the blue print of creation
Emblazoned is thy cosmic seal
This whole drama of life,
A projection of your magic dream.

Om with every breath and thought
Sets yogi free from karma
Giving nirvana to those who strive
As per their personal dharma.

Even the evil chanting Om
Are tainted not by karma
Would like a lotus lying,
In water unwetted and undying.

Absorbed in nada, the Bindu still !
By ceaseless ayam of prana
When Prana is still, Bindu is still,
Then conquer death, new life fulfill

As long as pran flows in Sharir
Jiwatma doth therein reside
Pran Leaves, Jiva leaves dehasthan
So live for God ! do pranayam.

Yogi death free, fearless bold
Prana between the eyebrows hold
By kevali in Shiv Netra be !
Oh death, where is thy victory ?

From fear of kala death they say
Gods, Sages in pranayam stay
But we must put this fear away
And live in prana the kevali way.

The human pran by rechaka goes
Thirty six fingers it outflows
Same length it takes to be inhaled
The living mystery still unveiled.

By pran the nadis purify
Toxins cleanse secretions dry
Then only can, you hold breaths gale
Mystery of life and death unveil.

In lotus posture yogi stay
Do sun moon pran of night and day
Sushmana Spinal Breathing called,
Victor of death be breath enthralled.

Yogi death free, fearless bold
Prana between the eyebrows hold
By kevali in Shiv Netra be !
Oh death, where is thy victory ?

Through surya nadi having filled
The prana of life in dhyan inhale
By kumbakh fill in stomach hold
By Chandra left apan exhale.

Meditate on radiant mass of light
In Manipur the navel chakra
The mystic sun and moon unite,
Find peace in Hamsa's deathless flight.

Merging our pran in His all Prana
Sun, moon and stars He holds
Our lives fuse with His livingness
Ourselves as Om in Him behold ! ! !

Om Tat Sat Om

Samadhi

O Thou phantom of creation's song
Why did you keep me tied so long?

    This nature's Eve, she can't deceive
    The people pure and strong
    For they in God's own light perceive
    The truth where they belong.

I stop this breath,
my stillness enters
Into the velvety darkness
of death.

    I grow
    in consciousness sublime
    Engulfing countries,
    continents and time.

I further grow
in omniscient glow
To unite with
maya's karmic flow.

The subtle laws
of cause and effect
Within myself
I do detect.

Beyond the gates of death!
I glide – untied;
Into regions sublime – surpassing
causation space and time.

Here Eternal Bliss is King
by name of Sat Chit Anand
Whose Life Sublime of Truth Divine
is Loving Brahmanand.

I fill immensity of space – I am
the Self Supreme
Looking down I do perceive
creation as a dream.

I then blend in the everlasting
vast expanse of Light
Becoming one with the
Cosmic Hum of all resounding
Oooommmmm.

Joy of Festivals

in Dhyan

An outsider here, I belong to a country
Where there is no life nor death
All 12 months I drink the divine elixir (Amrit)
Which awakens me to Self
Soul and dissolves my ego.
Oh Divine! My very being is ego's non being!

A foreigner to this land my true home belongs,
Where the blossoms of spring bloom every day;
In this body garden the 7 lotuses bloom
To adorn the lotus feet of Goraksha Nath.
Oh Soul! The lotuses become
the arches of the Divine feet!

A foreigner to this land I belong to a country
Where the festival of colours (Holi)
is celebrated each day.
There sprayed with 7 colours I am transformed
Whirling in festive joy
I become (colourless) pure white.
Oh! Brother oblivious of my ego & body.

An outsider here my true country is
Where there is perpetual irradiant splendour
Seven coloured wheels
            of mystic fire swirl within me
And every day is the festival of Divali (lights).

An outsider here the country
I belong to is where the music of
The 36 soothing ragas is heard
At Dessaraha the big drum sounds Nada Brahm
And the Ragas reverberate the Omkar.

I am a dweller of that boundless country
Where Lord Goraksha is King of all souls.
There he breathes the Ham Sah
we are being breathed
He does the work all sit at rest
Oh! Brother we all sit in tranquillity.

I am a dweller of that divine land
Which is called the Param Dhaia (Supreme Abode)
Siddha Nath is my name
My place town of rest
is Amrit Ghat (nectar vessel above third eye).

ALAKH NIRANJAN KAR SHIV OM

Appendix

Yogiraj SatGurunath Siddhanath

A brief introduction to his teachings

His Life

Yogiraj Sat Gurunath was born on May 10th, 1944. He is a Siddha by birth and belongs to one of the premier families of Gwalior, India. Educated in Sherwood College [Nainital], he spent his early years in the Himalayas with the great Nath Yogis, in whose presence he was transformed. The Divine Transformation was completed by his deep and personal experience with Mahavtar Babaji (Shiva-Goraksha-Nath Babaji) – the same immortal introduced by Yogananda in his classic, 'Autobiography of a Yogi'. Yogiraj is a direct disciple of Babaji and with his blessings has founded the Siddhanath Yoga Parampara.

Yogiraj now teaches various ancient forms of Yoga founded by the Nath Tradition, such as Mahavatar Babaji Kriya Yoga. He bestows powerful Shaktipat transmissions and unique 'Thought Free' Sates of Raja Yoga which empower the practitioners to gradually go into Samadhi (awareness of one's own Self), experiencing the depths of Eternal Being. Lord Krishna's vision has given him to realize the oneness of all yogas, faiths and religions.

His Genius

Besides the Himalayan Masters, SatGurunath is the only Siddha known to us and broadly accessible, who gives authentic experiences of Shaktipat Kundalini Energy Transmission created specifically for spiritual and healing transformation essential to the awakening and continued evolution of humankind. The sincere will receive these dimensions of the Guru's consciousness through direct experience as to what true yoga is rather than through intellectual exploration. The experience of SatGurunath's Consciousness will be bestowed as the Guru guides the seeker in transforming his thought-filled finite mind into infinite consciousness free of thoughts.

Herein lies the Genius of Gurunath - with a flash he bestows upon you His Consciousness of Natural Enlightenment, transforming the ripples of thought in your mind's lake into a waveless lake of Soul Awareness bereft of thought. With flawless clarity during this passage he keeps intact the awareness of ones individual self as the boundaries of it's I-ness melt into the knowing of one's own boundless Awareness. This process he calls "Shivapat".

The mind's I-ness will resist its soul consciousness expanding into super consciousness out of fear of losing its ego identity. But this is not the truth. The complete truth is that the individual mind loses its identity only to partake its vaster identity as infinite awareness, the drop merges into the ocean not to lose itself but to become of it.

Panapat is the Uniqueness of Gurunath where with utter simplicity by breathing through us he brings to you Shiv Goraksha Babaji's Kriya Yoga and the Timeless Yoga of the Nath Yogis. He has simplified the arduous Nath techniques, yet preserved the effectiveness of the sacred practices. As a living master, he offers to humanity his own clear-mind consciousness. In sharing this experience with each individual seeker personally and with thousands of receptive people the world over simultaneously, Sat Gurunath as "The Presence" reveals the secret that at the level of pure consciousness all Humanity is One.

The Nath Lineage of Kriya Yoga

As we peer into the akashic records of the misty past we get a glimpse of the lineage of the Nath Yogis. It began from Adi Nath, Lord Shiva Himself, who gave it to His consort Parvati, Uday Nath. She gave it to Vishnu - Santosh Nath, Ganesh and Nandi Nath. Then Lord Krishna as Vishnu initiated Lord Vivasvat, the Spirit of our Sun. The lineage was later guarded by the Kings of the Solar Dynasty: Vaivasvat Manu, King Ikshavaku down to Harishchandra, then to Lord Raghu Nath (Rama), 47th in descent from Ikshavaku. He is the 8th Rudra, esoterically connected with Shiv Goraksha Babaji, who is an incarnation of Lord Shiva Himself. It is through this grand lineage of the Nath Yogis that the royal science of Kriya Yoga has been preserved and handed down through the corridors of time by the ever-living Shiva- Goraksha-Babaji. It is to this lineage that Yogiraj Gurunath belongs – blessed by Babaji to spread this divine science in the East and West.

His Hallmark : The Knowing of a True Master

A Satguru or Empowering Master can be known by three distinct graces he bestows upon his disciples.
   •Transmit – center to center in their pranic chakras – the evolutionary Kundalini Energy: **Shaktipat**
     •Breathe the powerful breath through the breathing of disciples in their Spinal channels: **Pranapat**
     •Impart his consciousness of thought free enlightenment to the receptive: **Shivapat**
Only a Master who showers all three blessings on truth seekers is a true Satguru. Gurunath bestows all three blessings.

Wings to Freedom – The Journey of the Soul

The way of the white swan is the evolution of human conscious-ness, the most comprehensive enterprise ever undertaken by hu-manity, besides which the greatest of human achievements pale into insignificance. This process is Yoga, which commends itself to the foremost minds of East and West. In the human brain ex-ists the lateral ventricles in the shape of a "Swan in Flight" with its head pointing to the back as though the swan is flying faster than light back to the future. When the Hamsa Yogi, through meditation and pranayam, activates the Kundalini energy, then these ventricles in the brain open up. The two petals in the Agya Chakra, corresponding to the pituitary gland, open. The Yogi, at this stage, experiences Hamsa Consciousness, being breathed by the Divine Indweller.

The Sushumna channel in the spinal chord is the highway through which the Kundalini Energy travels and the evolution of consciousness takes place. It is the kinetic energy remain-ing after the completion of the universe. This force lies as light/ sound vibrations potentially coiled around the swayambhu linga in the mooladhar chakra. To avail of it for one's own evolution and realization is the birthright of every human soul. It may be awakened by yogic procedures - best by Unmani, a no-mind state of absorption.

As the Hamsa Nath Yogi progresses in the Hamsa meditation, the third eye opens up in the Agya Chakra and he goes into the Sarvikalpa consciousness. Then, by further practice, he pene-trates the Star of the Eye and expands to the Paramahamsa Nath Yogi state of Nirvikalpa consciousness, dwelling in the Cave of Brahma , the brain's third ventricle. Then his awareness evolves further beyond the I-ness of humanity to settle in the lateral swan-like ventricles of the brain, where he becomes the Siddha

Nath Yogi. The mighty Hamsa soul has won its wings to freedom. As the subtle fibers of the Corona Radiata light up with Divine effulgence he takes flight into Cosmic consciousness as the Avadhoot Nath Yogi. He experiences the total Divinity of and beyond creation, gaining the ultimate knowledge of "Tat Tvam Asi" - "That Thou Art". The Yogi then merges into Niranjan, the final Nirvana, having attained the enlightenment of Buddha and Christ. This Avadhoot Nath Yogi returns to the world no more. If, under rare circumstances, he ever does, it will be the descent of Divinity as Avatar Nath Yogi.

SatGurunath's Vision for World Peace
Hear Our Soul Call!

If World Peace is to Herald the Dawn of a New Age, realize that
Humanity Our Uniting Religion
Breath Our Uniting Prayer and
Consciousness Our Uniting God

Earth Peace Through Self Peace

SatGurunath works tirelessly to
transform
his myriad worldwide students

More Books
By
Yogiraj Gurunath Siddhanath

Books by Yogiraj Gurunath Siddhanath

Earth Peace Through Self Peace

Grasp this splendid and unique opportunity to be enlightened by the wisdom of a Realized Master of Yoga. Gurunath speaks not from the learning of books, but from his own direct experience, in his own simple, direct way, clearing away all doubts and irrelevancies.

Wings to Freedom

Mystic revelations from the immortal Babaji and other Himalayan Yogis, as experienced by a perfected Master, Yogiraj SatGurunath Siddhanath. Follow his footsteps and experience through his words, as he walks his talk, in the jungles, temples, ashrams and hidden [to the uninitiated] spiritual vortices of India. Enrich your life with the secret oral traditions revealed for the first time - mysteries of life, immortality and the attainment of Self-Realization.

Babaji The Lightning Standing Still

This is the most in depth exposition of the the greatest enigmatic mystery of spiritual myth, legend and history, called Babaji in recent times and Gorakshanath in the ancient times. Yogiraj calls Him,'the Non-Being Essentiality.'

Shiva-Goraksha-Babaji is the ever appearing disappearing star of salvation to all humans and celestials alike. He is the lightning standing still who transforms himself into the star each time a soul is enlightened.

Yogiraj was personally transformed and enlightened by Babaji and is able to reveal the many hidden dimensions of this glorious Being.

Yoga Patanjal

For thousands of years, the yoga sutras attributed to Rishi Patanjali has been the premier text for all those who aspired to understand the spiritual evolution of consciousness towards Self-Realization. Yogiraj, from his own experience, has offered an illuminating commentary that stands unique in the annals of yogic tradition wherein he has been able to reveal hidden aspects of the original terse text.